Excerpts from Life

Soraya Renae

BookLeaf Publishing

India | USA | UK

Presentation by *BookLeaf Publishing*

Web: www.bookleafpub.com

E-mail: info@bookleafpub.com

ISBN: 9789360948948

First edition 2024

See The Sea

To the vastness of the sea
There is no see.

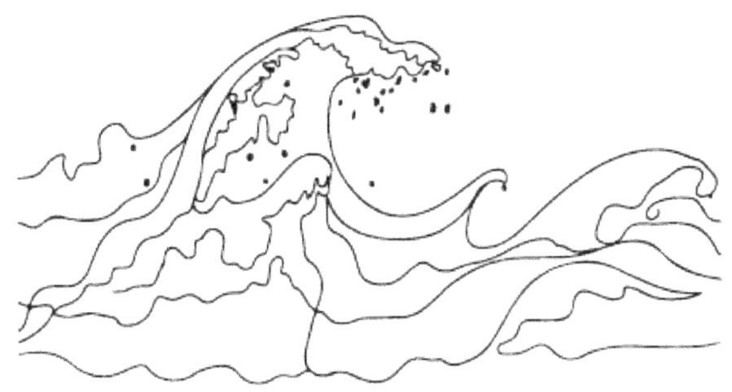

The Secrets of the World

Lo and behold
The blue of the sea

Lo and behold
The green of the trees

Lo and behold
The gray of the sky

Lo and behold
The colors of the wild
The wind of the world
The sway, the peace, the storm
The shades of the world

Is it brown,
Is it gray,
Is the mountain going to say

Is it blue
Is it green
Is the sea going to sway

Will the sea whisper its secrets
Or will it bury it deep within?

I try hard to hear the words
But only whispers come
So low and pure that
Lo and behold
I feel the comprehension at bay.

Selfless Women

The expectation is high
The expectation is normal
The expectation is selfless

A selfless woman is expected
A selfless woman is normal
A selfless woman is ordained by society

But is a woman born selfless?

Women are not born selfless
They are made selfless

Man, made selfless woman
Selfless women made selfless women.

Red and White

Going darker redder
Growing bitter

The part of the tall
The moment to ponder

How did it come
What did we miss
When did we take it for granted
I wonder

Red on the outside
White inside
Goes yellow after a while
Then brown takes over

But my eyes are big enough
The nose smells it
My hands capture it
And yet I wonder
How did it come into being

So it is hard a little
But it is sweet in tons
For every bite
Just blasts into my mind

For never again
I take it for granted.

Move In And Out

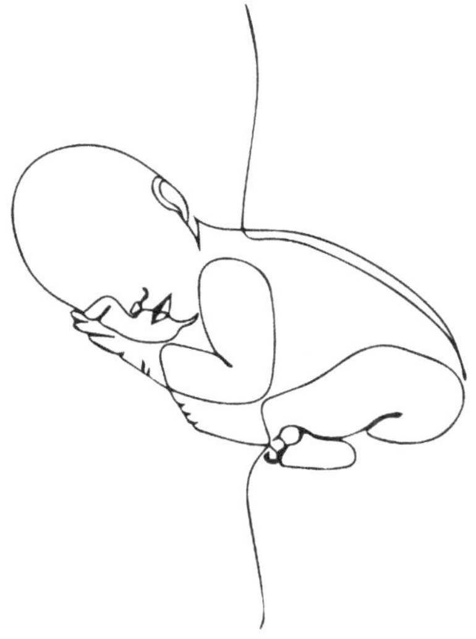

Only ten months into the world
He looks and hears all day long
He observes the world with his little beautiful
eyes.

But it is weird to observe
What the two-months-old observes.

He stays lying, watching, waving
In his ramp, laughing and crying
And all the while seeing around

Here comes a giant
And there goes another giant
One giant from one point to another
And then another giant from another point to the
other

There are times when the giants stop
Boom out for a while
Stop for a while
Sometimes sit
Play with the kid
Then again they move on
Going from one point to another

The ten-months-old does the same
Moving from one point to another
They hold something
They bring something
They take something
They do not own anything.

Now the ten-months-old grows
He can walk, hold, grab and let go
Now he does the same
Holds out and moves on
Moves in and out, all day around

The grind will go on
All day and time around.

Imagined Monster

The monster of the imagined world
Creeps in the darkest of night
I am normal most of the time
The monster creeps in the loneliest of times
No one saw it in the darkest of times
Thus no one believes most of the time

They say,
It is all in the mind
It is not true most of the time
It is imagined

It is false
It is just another stall

All true, all true, I say
Go away, you monster, I say
At the darkest of times
Yet the monster creeps in the loneliest of times

Loved ones suggest many ways
One comes with a packet of feel-good cards
One comes with a glass of milk
One comes with a sack of stories
One keeps coming
With a trick

I try, I try, everything they spray
Go away, you monster, I say
At the darkest of times
Yet the monster creeps in the loneliest of times.

I Click and Click

In the deep dark mass
The colors are vast

Thousands of hours of money
Could not even come close to it

The lenses and the edits
Could not even predict
The beauty that exists

I see the blue
The white and hue

I see the green
The glitter and serene

Yet I click and click
But none persists

So I decide,
As is every time
To stow away the device

Sit there soaking in
All colors and sounds

Weird, scary, vast, or exciting
Be it any or all
I sit with my eyes hovering around

As the time has gone
And there remains no picture of it
I am afraid of forgetting them soon

But behold the mind of mine
Doesn't remember what I saw
Just the colors
Just the feelings
Just the sounds

Tell me my friends how can I now pronounce

How do I tell you the beauty of it
How do I convince you of the worth of it
I have no picture but the memory of it

The picture my friends captured exists
But they are bytes of it
The fragmented pieces do not convey
The feeling of it.

Feed the Ego

Love me, I say
Love me, I cry
In the quietest whisper

Love me, I plead
Adorn me, I squeak
In the humblest of times

When I walk, you gawk
When I cry, you turn
When I sit, you sigh

Give all to my fire
Give need to my feed
Give likes to my peeks

Listen to all I say
Feed all you have to my ego

I ask for love again
For love to bejewel me
Because everyone owes me
To feed my ego.

Discipline

My heart pumps the blood
In and out
Day and night
Time and again

Yet why is it hard for me
To emulate the same discipline
Time and again?

My heart is pumping the blood
In and out
Never stopping

Such a small part of the whole
Yet disciplined the most

Listens to none, works a ton
Neither bows down nor complains

And here I am sleeping on a small
inconvenience
Yet the heart pumps
In and out
Even when broken into pieces

How naive I am looking for inspiration outside
When my own heart
The epitome of discipline
Breathes in and out

It is breathing
It is kicking
It is pumping

Be it rain
Be it strain
It moves like a non-stop train

When the mind frails
When hand stays
When legs don't sway
Listen to the thump
Get the groove
And move on and on

Day in and day out
Pump in and pump out
If the heart can, so can I

Broken into pieces and still can go on
Go on and go out
Go for all
Pump in and pump out
Heart for all

Bewitched

You have bewitched me
My body and soul

You have attached me
My hand and whole

I sleep or I ride
It is you to whom I abide

I eat or drink
It is for you, I blink

Yet I wonder if there is a spell
That breaks the swell

Will time be the test?
Will someone break the spell?

Will I work against me
Or will someone come to rescue?

No, no more
Says my heart

Be it for a while or whole
I will stay loyal to you

Be it you or me
I will stay for you

Be it time or tide
Be it rhythm or roll
Be it magic or fusion

I am bewitched by you
Your body and soul

When the Perfect Hits

In goes the time
Out comes nothing

In goes the steps
Out comes nothing

Day in and day out
It is the same around

But then there are days
When the sun shines ablaze

There is light
There is not a mere slight
All is going right and bright

The chest puffs up
The steps perk up

The mouth smiles
The heart vibes

It goes a while
Only to turn vile

The perfect in you
Comes to haunt you

Takes away the smiles
Makes the sun's demise

First, there are clouds
Then comes the rain

Soon the storm takes everything away

It makes small victories big
Never to try harder again

Only if you knew there is always a change

Never has anything remained the same
Never will anything remain the same

Say this when the sun shines
Repeat it when the worlds collide

The Expected Change

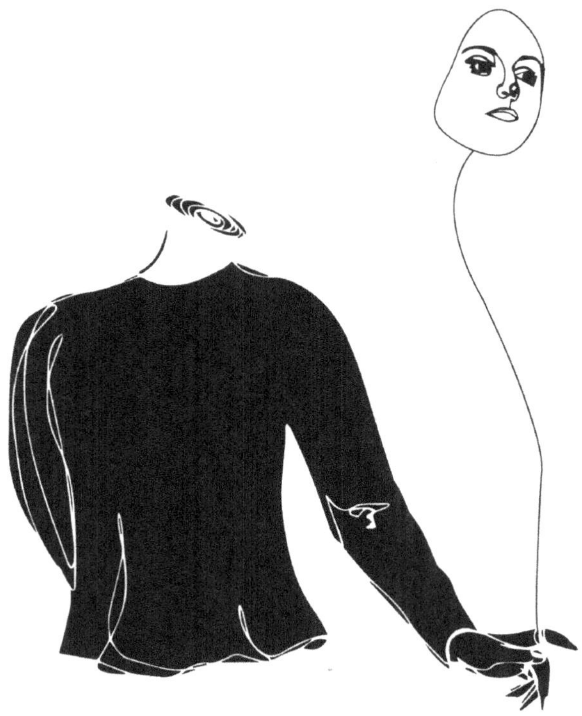

In the prime of life
They search for exotics

In the wilderness
They find the one

Their different way of thinking
Their different way of seeing

Their different way of living
Attracts them and keeps them

Their difference to oneself
Is this the key to their fall?

They intertwine the differences
Finding and biding time for themselves

Promises are made to never change
Promises are made to love their way

But then the sacred chants
Uttered in the presence of thousands
Change the entire history

Their differences become hindrances
Their uniqueness becomes arrogance

Be a little adaptive
Change a little perspective
Work along the majority

For a day or two you resist
Then you insist
One day you only exist

Adaptation prevails
Majority wins

You become a family

Was it wrong to resist?
Was it wrong to reject the change?
Was it wrong to ask?

Adaption for the sake of others
Is the first learning for a woman

But where are the humans
Making it adaptable for women

We keep losing our identities
First for a day and then forever

They say it is just for a day
Will you be anyone else even for a second

The empty nods go in unison
But when the time comes they scatter in derision

Many times you lose the debate
Because you do not know
What should be the end
You know if the current is right or wrong
You do not know if the next is bearable or not

How far the stick will bend
Before the snap comes

The unknown is the demon
The evil one wishes to avoid

Whom to tell
Whom to fight

The one for whom
Your uniqueness was divine
Now asks for the same to be at bay

Never ever a woman has said
Life has been better
Coming out of the same terrain

They complain in close circles
One to one to their peers
But never dare to be unique because
That gets them out of the herd

Knowledge becomes the enemy
When there is no desired end
Your fight is futile
When there are unknown terrains

Can I be a Writer?

I am looking at the paper
With a brown patch and blank ink

I wish I could see it meaning behind
The time the writer felt it in his mind

Did he think it through
Before going through
Or let the words slide
All at one time

Wonder it is that a few can write
What a lot of people can understand
Yet the meaning is lost
For the most
Unfortunate sometimes
With the lines

I wonder if one will ever satisfy
The hunger for meaning
Or getting inspired for living

I wish I could be with the writer
When he writes
Will he reveal his secrets
Or be as discreet as his lines

I wish I could be a writer
But I wonder
If something will ever materialize.

30

Librarian Recommends

Read this they say
For getting wisdom of the sage
Read that they say
For getting wisdom of the old age

Subscribe to the reading list of your lifetime
Read this and read that
Read the thousands of lists that talk about the
best of all times
Subscribe to the upcoming nominations, await
the wins

Then read this and of course, you need to read
that

But I am the fool for finding books in the pool
The old ways are the best
When you don't know where your destiny rests

The old man behind the desk
Hidden behind the decks
Face buried behind a book
Has the most distinctive look

Why wouldn't he be happy
Surrounded by stories and reading jolly
Sees a fellow reader
Jumps with excitement for the hunt

How amazing he is at his job
When all is lost
He looks into the box
Pulls out books
Says I would like the most
Never has he been wrong
Maybe once or twice, in long

How amazing, life is right now
One person, all the lists and recommendations
Tell me exactly what I need to read next

I wish I had Words To Describe

Every fight turns into tears
More from me than yours

I twist and turn more than you
I sleep less compared to you
And I love you more than me

You tower over me
Based on how much outgoing you are

You tower over me
Based on how many friends you have got

You are relaxed
I am a storm
You are calm
I am a mess all around

You remain fit
I get fits

Anger, irritation, tension and blues
They are my companions all day through

You say I have changed
I know that babe
But you talk more than you listen
And you fix more than you amend

I wish I had words
To tell you
How much it hurts me
But I fail at every instance

I read to learn words
Words I could use
To make you understand
How much it hurts me
In the words, you will understand.

Wants and Fails

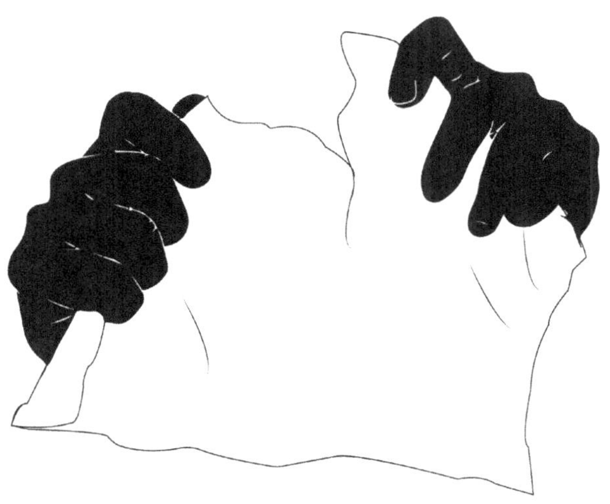

He came and rushed about
He trimmed and cleaned up
He packed and had lunch

He is handsome as hell
He is polite as well
He is amazing and he is mine

Yet he is going away
Only for a couple of days
He wanted me to come
But I had to shun

There was no way
I could go away
I have to stay
There is no way

It is the time I need
To work on my deed
I need to lose weight
I need to get in the game

He does not know
He is not aware
I do not know
How to tell him all

I want to lose weight
I want to look great
I have tried for a while
Failed with every try

This is one more try
But I want to do it on my own
He is supportive I know
But I am scared if I fail
It will cause a dent

But I know he will get to know
Not in the beginning I suppose
But once I have come to know

What it will be like for me
For the next couple of weeks

Once I get going
Once I see the result
Then the time will come
I will wait for him to notice

Wouldn't it be great
When he sees it himself
Notices the change
Wouldn't he be surprised
Wouldn't it be great

But I know I will fall through
He will know before the sun is through
The day will go as it has done before
But will there be any change
In love and the air.

An Urge to Stop and Wonder

No research and no reading
Yet their voice is the loudest

Only shout and fists smoking the sky
With no work on the ground

No respect and no humility
Only empty words
Voicing an unknown entity

Too timid to think
Too short on time
Deaf and blind to their own mind

A wise looks a fool to them
A polite looks a tool to them
A humble is a liar

A wonder is a satire

They speak else's mind
They repeat like a parrot's tongue
They close the curtains tight
They follow the sensational
They diss the emotional
They call out the sane ones
They blow away the wise ones

Hard like rice
They pay no heed to the wise
Unless boiled to the core
To soften and listen to the wise

They realise the truth
Only to say "oooo"
Humble and humility still at bay
Squashed to their bone
Forgotten and left alone

But some survive
Come to the other side
Know the power of change
Become more open to the words
Build the mind of their own
Learn the values of change
Learn the power of thinking, analysing and
debating

Learn the power of learning

Become kind
Become forgiving
Become humble
Look at their old selves with heavy hearts
Urge the ones like them to mend their ways
Give their own examples to deaf ears
Show them the ones who got squashed
But fail with many of them

The wise move on
They work
They remain consistent
They learn to learn
They hold true to their values
But now and then they show their work

The learned is a critic
The learned voices the vices and virtue
But never goes beyond the work
The judgment on work never marks the
personality

The curve is hard to master
The river is hard to cross
Yes those who do are calmer

So fellow beings

For once shut your mouth
And open your mind
Think for once that you know nothing
Tackle like a child
Try once for yourself
For your fellow beings
And for once
For the love of God
Speak out something sensible
Before you face the lightning.

Trapped

Oh, look! This is good
I wonder what's next?
That looks good
Oh, her life is good

I scroll and scroll
I roll and roll
I judge and judge
I want and want

Oh, look at the time
Just stop
Look at the pile
Oh, this is beautiful

I scroll and scroll
I close and open
I like and comment
I lack and lack

Oh, look! He is back from work
He did the work
He spoke to real people
Oh, he looks satisfied

I roll and roll
I watch and hit next
I search for the song
I sing along

Oh, look! Family video call
Saw them ages ago
Have nothing to talk
Oh, look it disconnected

I judge and judge
I know she is rich
I know he is a snob
I know they own it all

Oh, look! I am sad
Again, again and again
Day after day
Oh, look everyone is happy

I want and want
I want the car she has
I want the money they have
I want the life he has

Oh, look! This is sad
I scroll and scroll
I want and want
Oh, I am trapped and trapped

Bee and A Two-Year-Old

The buzzing, the woozing
The bees and their humming

It buzzes, it hymns
It moves a thousand times
It nears, it moves round and round
It circles the deity around

The same old insanity
For the deity
The same old humming
For the honey

To the old eyes
It is the same old story
The bee and the flower
Going merry-go-round

But dear reader wait for a while
Here comes the two-year-old
With all smiles and daisies
Laughing
Clapping
Falling
Jumping
Dancing
At the scene

Dear reader let us see the scene

Here is a bee
Shaking its bottom
Dancing
Entertaining
Enticing

Let us go a little further
And we can see the romance

The art of seduction
In the purest of stance

The flower you can hear
Reeling with expectation
If you listen close
It is laughing and crackling

The bee dances
Round and round
Finally the flower
Can take no more
It begs the bee to stop
Urges to take the pay
And dance no more

It says come again
When I am laughing no more
But for now, let us not continue anymore

The bee takes the pay
Gives a final bow and flys away

Merrily flying towards the home
When at last it meets the queen
It pays her the day's work
Whose smile makes it worthwhile

Now the bee sleeps
Dreaming of the laughter it received
But the dream is mixed with another smile
Of the two-year-old
Who stood awhile

Now reader come back to the two-year-old
He is still telling about the bee

To whomever will listen
He enacts and laughs
He loves the life of it all

Though now he says something wise
That a bee dances
With no music in sight
The buzz if you hear is its music
As the laughter of mine

He laughs more and enacts again
Till he is tired and could keep up no more

He will wake up tomorrow
To run to the flower
To wait for the bee
To see the dance
To laugh some more

Dear reader, do not part away
As I have one request to make
We took a lot of space from them
Let us make sure to make some space again

A space for the flowers to bloom
A space for the bees to come
A space for the two-year-old to gaze
A space for the old to live again.

Journey towards Hope

I miss the world when I was young
Not the kind where age was just a number

Okay I lie
There was no such time

In the beginning, there was no memory
Later came the proudness of the skin
Soon it was the rank in exams
I was climbing up the rock

Then the world took a turn
The throne was destroyed

For days there was no night
There were no colours
Only the shades of black

Days and years
Years and decades
The darkness lingers
Making it impossible to linger

Is there hope?
Is there hope?
Is there hope?

Every day is the same question
Some days the answers are yes
Some days the answers are maybe

But since it has not been no yet
Means there is something
I am hoping for
Maybe a miracle
Of my lifetime.

Try one Once

There are multiple cures for hate,
Off the top of my head:
Love,
Kindness,
Empathy,
Nature,
Breathe,
Walking,
Sleeping,
Eating cake,

Pick one
Or make one,
Or find one,
Give a try,
Give a fair chance,
For once.

9 789360 948948